TOEFL iBT® Basics

TOEFL iBT® テストスキル入門
~VOAで学ぶ四技能のストラテジー~

津田晶子 ▶ Akiko Tsuda
クリストファー・ヴァルヴォーナ ▶ Chris Valvona
金志佳代子 ▶ Kayoko Kinshi
岩本弓子 ▶ Yumiko Iwamoto

NAN'UN-DO

TOEFL iBT® Basics

Copyright©2015
by

Akiko Tsuda
Chris Valvona
Kayoko Kinshi
Yumiko Iwamoto

All Rights Reserved.

No part of this book may be reproduced in any form without written permission from the authors and Nan'un-do Co., Ltd.

TOEFL iBT is a registered trademark of Educational Testing Service (ETS).
This publication is not endorsed or approved by ETS.

Preface

Founded in 1942, Voice of America (VOA) is now the largest U.S. International Broadcaster, with approximately 1,800 hours of radio and television programming transmitted each week to about 134 million people around the world. VOA broadcasts news and features, with a stated aim that it "will present the policies of the United States clearly and effectively," and that the news will be "accurate, objective, and comprehensive." (from the VOA Charter, 1976)

VOA also has a special "Learning English" language section. In this textbook, we have selected 15 articles from the area of "Words and Their Stories." Each article presents unusual English expressions and idioms, and explains their meaning and the often fascinating stories of how they came into usage. The textbook is therefore divided into 15 units, and each unit centers around one article.

In the units, not only will students have a chance to read and listen to these stimulating articles, they will also learn new vocabulary, develop note-taking skills, practice shadowing, and answer comprehension questions specifically designed in the style of the TOEFL® test. Furthermore, students will answer TOEFL-style essay questions, while receiving pointers on how to structure and write their essays.

Therefore, by going through this textbook, students will learn interesting stories about how parts of the English language came to be, and will also hone their skills for TOEFL success!

はじめに

　本書 *TOEFL iBT® Basics* は、初めて TOEFL を受ける学生や、将来、語学研修や留学を目指す学生を対象に、Voice of America (VOA) を素材にして、四技能のテストストラテジーを学ぶ入門者向けの教材です。本書は全 15 ユニットで構成され、1 ユニットで 1 テーマが完結します。また、各ユニットの内容構成は次のとおりです。

I Words and Phrases

このユニットで出てくる重要表現を学びます。

II Note-taking

本文を聴きながら、ノートを取りましょう。日本語でも英語でも構いません。

III Reading Aloud & Shadowing

CD を聴きながら、発音に気をつけて音読をし、次に本を閉じて、シャドーイングしましょう。淀みなく読めるようになるまで、何度も繰り返して練習しましょう。

IV Reading Comprehension

TOEFL iBT® の問題形式を意識したリーディング問題です。レベル・ニーズに応じて、Extension Activity 1（速読）、Extension Activity 2（タイピング）にも挑戦してみてください。

V Integrated Skills

質問文について、ディクテーションをします。そのあと、同じ問題について、今度は自分だったらどう答えるか、Extension Activity 3（Writing）、Extension Activity 4（Speaking）に取り組んでみましょう。

TOEFL® Test Skills

TOEFL iBT® の受験に際してのアドバイスやキャンパス用語などの語彙を紹介します。

　本書によって、皆さんが四技能のテストスキルを身につけ、TOEFL® 対策のストラテジーを学ぶきっかけづくりになれば幸いです。最後になりましたが、本書の作成にあたり、南雲堂の丸小雅臣氏には企画段階から大変お世話になりました。また、パイロット版作成については、國崎倫先生、ケリー・マクドナルド先生に貴重なご意見をいただきました。この場を借りて心からお礼を申し上げます。

津田晶子
クリストファー・ヴァルヴォーナ
金志佳代子
岩本弓子

CONTENTS

Preface III

はじめに IV

Unit 1   **From Couch Potato to Cabin Fever** 6

Unit 2   **Fireworks!** 12

Unit 3   **We Put Things in "Apple Pie Order"** 18

Unit 4   **The Big Easy and Sin City** 24

Unit 5   **Bigwig** 30

Unit 6   **Grapevine** 36

Unit 7   **Quit Buggin' Me!** 42

Unit 8   **It's Not Worth a Hill of Beans!** 48

Unit 9   **What's a GI Joe?** 54

Unit 10   **Great Scott** 60

Unit 11   **Swan Song** 66

Unit 12   **When Is a Choice Not Really a Choice?** 72

Unit 13   **Baloney** 78

Unit 14   **Mayday** 84

Unit 15   **Without Them, Machines Fall Apart** 90

Glossary 97

Unit 1　From Couch Potato to Cabin Fever

I Words and Phrases

この章で学ぶ表現を確認しましょう。

A 語群からもっとも適切な5つの語句を選びましょう。

1. 機器　　（　　　　　）　　2. カーソル　　（　　　　　　）
3. 支える　（　　　　　）　　4. まゆ、ねぐら（　　　　　　）
5. 用語　　（　　　　　）

| term | device | cursor | cocoon | hold |

B 左側の単語の反対語を選びましょう。

1. boredom　　　⇔　　（　　　　　　　　　）
2. restlessness　⇔　　（　　　　　　　　　）
3. popular　　　⇔　　（　　　　　　　　　）

| uncommon | calmness | excitement |

6　TOEFL iBT® Basics

II. Note-taking

本文を聴きながらノートをとりましょう。(英語でも日本語でも構いません)

III. Reading Aloud & Shadowing

CDを聴きながら、発音に気をつけて音読をしましょう。次に本を閉じて、シャドーイングしましょう。

1. Some unusual words describe how a person spends his or her time.
2. A couch is a piece of furniture that people sit on while watching television.
3. Someone who likes to spend a lot of time sitting or lying down while watching television is sometimes called a couch potato.
4. Couch potatoes enjoy watching television just as mouse potatoes enjoy working on computers.

IV. Reading Comprehension

1 Some unusual words describe how a person spends his or her time. For example, someone who likes to spend a lot of time sitting or lying down while watching television is sometimes called a couch potato. A couch is a piece of furniture that people sit on while watching television. Robert Armstrong, an artist from California, developed the term couch potato in nineteen seventy-six. Several years later, he listed the term as a trademark with the United States government. Mister Armstrong also helped write a funny book about life as a full-time television watcher. It is called the "Official Couch Potato Handbook."

2 Couch potatoes enjoy watching television just as mouse potatoes enjoy working on computers. A computer mouse is the device that moves the pointer, or cursor, on a computer screen. The description of mouse potato became popular in nineteen ninety-three. American writer Alice Kahn is said to have invented the term to describe young people who spend a lot of time using computers.

3 Too much time inside the house using a computer or watching television can cause someone to get cabin fever. A cabin is a simple house usually built far away from the city. People go to a cabin to relax and enjoy quiet time. Cabin fever is not really a disease. However, people can experience boredom and restlessness if they spend too much time inside their homes. This is especially true during the winter when it is too cold or snowy to do things outside. Often children get cabin fever if they cannot go outside to play. So do their parents. This happens when there is so much snow that schools and even offices and stores are closed.

4 Some people enjoy spending a lot of time in their homes to make them nice places to live. This is called nesting or cocooning. Birds build nests out of sticks to hold their eggs and baby birds. Some insects build cocoons around themselves for protection while they grow and change. Nests and cocoons provide security for wildlife. So people like the idea of nests and cocoons, too. The terms cocooning and nesting became popular more than twenty years ago. They describe people buying their first homes and filling them with many things.

❺ These people then had children. Now these children are grown and have left the nest. They are in college. Or they are married and starting families of their own far away. Now these parents are living alone without children in their empty nest. They have become empty nesters.

(421 Words)

本文について、下記の設問に答えましょう。

1. The word **developed** in paragraph 1 is closest in meaning to
   a. narrowed
   b. matured
   c. revolved
   d. established

2. The word **description** in paragraph 2 refers to
   a. acceptance
   b. contribution
   c. depiction
   d. collection

3. In paragraph 1, what can be inferred about Robert Armstrong?
   a. He is a couch potato.
   b. He stopped working after 1976.
   c. He works for the United States government.
   d. He is a writer as well as an artist.

4. What does the author imply in paragraph 3?
   a. It's not good for you to spend too much time indoors.
   b. You should go to the hospital if you have cabin fever.
   c. Being inside for a long period of time is relaxing.
   d. Only children get cabin fever.

5. What types of people are NOT mentioned in the article?

   a. people who watch a lot of television
   b. people who use the computer a lot
   c. people who work hard to make their homes comfortable
   d. people who live with their parents even after they've grown up

【Extension Activity 1: timed reading】
１分間でどれだけ読めるか計測してみましょう。

| 1st time | words | | 2nd time | words |

【Extension Activity 2: typing】
１分間でどれだけタイプできるか計測してみましょう。

| 1st time | words | | 2nd time | words |

V Integrated Skills 〔4〕

Talk about an important national holiday in your home country. Describe it and explain why it is important.

CD を聴いて、(　　　　　) に記入しましょう。

　The most important national holiday in Japan is New Year's Day. This is because we believe that (1.　　　　　) is the start of everything, (2.　　　　　) the Buddhist belief. In Japan, the New Year is observed on January First, although (3.　　　　　) have new year's celebrations (4.　　　　　), following the lunar calendar.

　It is rather (5.　　　　　) and many people take several days off to spend time with their families, (6.　　　　　) called *osechi* at home. There are some who go abroad to (7.　　　　　) there.

(98 words)

【Extension Activity 3: writing】
あなた自身の答えを書いてみましょう。

....
....
....
....
....
....
....

【Extension Activity 4: speaking】
あなた自身の答えを話してみましょう。

TOEFL® Test Skills

TOEFL® と TOEIC® の違いについて

TOEIC®がビジネスコミュニケーション重視であるのに対し、TOEFL®は北米の大学で学ぶことができる英語力を測るテストであるため、アカデミックなボキャブラリーが多く出題されます。また、内容も、地理や歴史、自然科学、美術など、多岐にわたります。

コンピュータベースのiBTテストになってから、英語の四技能すべてを駆使できる能力が求められます。キーボード操作も必要ですので、タッチタイピング（画面を見ながら打つこと）ができると有利です。英文タイプの練習用のソフトウェアやウェブサイトが色々ありますので、自分に合ったものを探して練習しておきましょう。

Unit 2 Fireworks!

1 Words and Phrases

この章で学ぶ表現を確認しましょう。

A 語群からもっとも適切な5つの語句を選びましょう。

1. 宗教的な　（　　　　　）　2. 被告側　（　　　　　）
3. 恋人　　（　　　　　）　4. 爆発する（　　　　　）
5. 裁判官　（　　　　　）

| explode | religious | defense | judge | sweetheart |

B 左側の定義にあてはまるように、空所を埋めてみましょう。

1. someone whose profession is to provide people with legal advice
 (l _ _ _ er)
2. a series of games, sports events (co _ pet _ _ ion)
3. freedom from control by another country (inde _ _ _ dence)

12　TOEFL iBT® Basics

II Note-taking 🎧 5

本文を聴きながらノートをとりましょう。（英語でも日本語でも構いません）

III Reading Aloud & Shadowing 🎧 6

CDを聴きながら、発音に気をつけて音読をしましょう。次に本を閉じて、シャドーイングしましょう。

1. People use the expression "fireworks" throughout the year.

2. The Fourth of July is Independence Day in the United States.

3. Americans traditionally celebrate their nation's freedom with giant public parties and fireworks at night.

4. In Washington, large crowds gather near the Washington Monument to listen to music and watch a huge fireworks show.

IV Reading Comprehension

Reading

① The expression "fireworks" gets its meaning from the fireworks that people shoot into the sky when they are celebrating a great event. Rockets explode to fill the dark, night sky with bright reds and blues, with yellows and greens and whites.

② The expression also means a great show of noisy anger, or something exciting. For example, a defense lawyer in a court trial may become very emotional in arguing with the government lawyer about evidence affecting the accused. The judge finally stops the loud argument and calls the two lawyers forward. He tells them, "I want no more of these fireworks in my courtroom."

③ Another kind of fireworks can be any event or activity that is especially exciting. One such event is falling in love. If anything can produce fireworks, it is a sweetheart's kiss or the touch of a lover's hand. Often movie or television cartoons show fireworks to represent the excitement of a kiss.

④ People use the expression "fireworks" throughout the year. But if you live in the United States and want to see real fireworks, the best time of the year is about now. The Fourth of July is Independence Day in the United States. Americans traditionally celebrate their nation's freedom with giant public parties and fireworks at night. In Washington, for example, large crowds gather near the Washington Monument to listen to music and watch a huge fireworks show. In other cities and smaller towns, local people listen to band concerts and watch fireworks explode in a dark sky.

⑤ Many other countries around the world also enjoy the tradition of exploding fireworks on special days. In Australia, the city of Sydney begins each new year with a fireworks show at midnight. China is the birthplace of fireworks. Large fireworks shows were held often during earlier times in

China. Now, people use small fireworks to help celebrate weddings and birthdays.

❻ France also has a great fireworks tradition. A large fireworks show always takes place on Bastille Day, which celebrates the beginning of the French Revolution. The French city of Cannes holds an international fireworks competition each year in July and August. In India, people have been using fireworks for more than 500 years. A great Indian fireworks show takes place during the religious celebration of Diwali, every autumn.

(381 Words)

本文について、下記の設問に答えましょう。

1. The word **local** in paragraph 4 is closest in meaning to

　a. broad　　　**b.** liberal　　　**c.** countryside　　　**d.** neighborhood

2. The word **celebrates** in paragraph 6 is closest in meaning to

　a. mesmerizes　　**b.** blames　　**c.** commemorates　　**d.** overlooks

3. In paragraphs 1, 2, and 3, fireworks are NOT associated with

　a. kissing someone you love　　**b.** achieving a goal
　c. getting very angry　　**d.** celebrating a large occasion

4. According to paragraph 5, where do fireworks come from?

　a. Australia　　**b.** China　　**c.** France　　**d.** India

5. Look at the four options below and decide which one best summarizes the article. Incorrect answers either leave out or misrepresent essential information.

　a. Fireworks are very important in the United States, especially on the Fourth of July when they are used to celebrate the country's freedom.
　b. Fireworks show when people are angry, excited, and in love. In fact, fireworks are used to represent many emotions, as well as celebrations.

c. India was the first country to use fireworks 500 years ago, and since then they have become more and more popular around the world. They are always used as a form of celebration.

d. Around the world, fireworks have been used on special days for hundreds of years. These days, fireworks represent many things such as celebration, anger, excitement, and love.

【Extension Activity 1: timed reading】
1分間でどれだけ読めるか計測してみましょう。

| 1st time | words | 2nd time | words |

【Extension Activity 2: typing】
1分間でどれだけタイプできるか計測してみましょう。

| 1st time | words | 2nd time | words |

V Integrated Skills 🎧 7

Who is your favorite relative? Describe him/her and explain why.

CD を聴いて、(   ). に記入しましょう。

I really loved my grandmother. She was (1.   ) and was (2.   ), so I was a little bit afraid of her (3.   ). I admire her as a woman who had lived a hard life (4.   ). I learned the real history of my country from a living witness like her. She always seemed to try to (5.   ). I liked her positivity. She liked reading and I probably (6.   ). She passed away several years ago but (7.   ).

(101 words)

【Extension Activity 3: writing】

あなた自身の答えを書いてみましょう。

_____
_____
_____
_____
_____
_____
_____

【Extension Activity 4: speaking】

あなた自身の答えを話してみましょう。

TOEFL® Test Skills

キャンパス用語クイズ （Part 1）

以下は英語圏の大学でよく使われる単語・表現です。あてはまるものを選び、書きましょう。

1. 大学院　　（　　　　　　）
2. 学部生　（　　　　　　）
3. 奨学金　　（　　　　　　）
4. 宿泊施設（　　　　　　）
5. 研究助成金（　　　　　　）

research grant	accommodation
graduate school	undergraduate
scholarship	

Unit 3 We Put Things in "Apple Pie Order"

I Words and Phrases

この章で学ぶ表現を確認しましょう。

A 語群からもっとも適切な5つの語句を選びましょう。

1. 商人・貿易商 (　　　　　)　2. 上陸する (　　　　　)
3. 容器　　　 (　　　　　)　4. 探検家　 (　　　　　)
5. 神話　　　 (　　　　　)

| explorer | mythology | land | container | trader |

B (　) 内の指示に従って、単語を書きかえましょう。

1. god（「女神」の意味に）　→ _____
2. believe（名詞形に）　　　→ _____
3. threat（動詞形に）　　　 → _____

II Note-taking 🎧 8

本文を聴きながらノートをとりましょう。（英語でも日本語でも構いません）

III Reading Aloud & Shadowing 🎧 9

ＣＤを聴きながら、発音に気をつけて音読をしましょう。次に本を閉じて、シャドーイングしましょう。

1. At one time, the tomato was called a love apple.
2. Spain imported the tomato from South America after Spanish explorers had landed there.
3. Spain then exported the tomato to Morocco.
4. Italian traders carried it on to Italy.

IV Reading Comprehension

Reading

① Nobody is sure where and when the expression "apple pie order" began. Some say that Scottish and English writers used the expression a long time ago. Others say it first was used in the northeastern American states known as New England. The housewives of New England cut their apples in even slices. Then they filled pie pans with them in an organized way, row upon row. As one writer said, the women of New England loved to have everything in its place. This perhaps explains why it generally is believed that the expression "apple pie order" began in New England.

② Another old expression describes the opposite condition — wild disorder. That expression is "apple of discord". It comes from ancient mythology. The myth says that all the gods and goddesses were sitting around the table to celebrate the marriage of Thetis and Peleus. One of the goddesses — Discord — was a troublemaker. She threw a golden apple on the table to be given as a prize to the most beautiful goddess. It was not an easy decision to make. How could they choose among Juno, Minerva and Venus. Paris was given the task of deciding. He decided to give the golden apple to Venus. Juno and Minerva were very angry and threatened him. This, the myth says, began the long Trojan war.

③ At one time, the tomato was called a love apple. That was a mistake. This is how the mistake happened: In the sixteenth century, Spain imported the tomato from South America after Spanish explorers had landed there. Spain then exported the tomato to Morocco. Italian traders carried it on to Italy. The Italian name for the tomato was "pomo di Moro" — apple of the Moors.

④ When French growers imported it from Italy, they thought "di Moro" meant "d'amour" — the French word for love. And so "pomo di Moro" became the apple of love. People believe many things about the apple. One belief is that it has great powers of keeping people healthy. A very common expression is "an apple a day keeps the doctor away." Another belief is based on fact. The expression is "one rotten apple spoils the barrel." When an apple begins to go bad, it ruins all the other apples around it in the container. The expression has come to mean that one bad person in a group can cause everyone to act bad.

(397 Words)

本文について、下記の設問に答えましょう。

1. The word **disorder** in paragraph 2 is closest in meaning to
    a. disobey
    b. complaint
    c. ailment
    d. confusion

2. The word **common** in paragraph 4 refers to
    a. simplified
    b. prevalent
    c. refined
    d. valuable

3. According to paragraph 1, what can be said about the women of New England?
    a. They cut their apples into too many slices.
    b. They didn't enjoy cooking.
    c. They liked to have everything well-organized.
    d. They needed more apples for their pies.

4. According to paragraph 3, where did the tomato originally come from?
    a. South America
    b. Spain
    c. Italy
    d. France

5. Expressions using "apple" can mean all of the following EXCEPT
    a. a tomato
    b. order and organization
    c. disorder and craziness
    d. lack of health

【Extension Activity 1: timed reading】

1分間でどれだけ読めるか計測してみましょう。

| 1st time _____ words | 2nd time _____ words |

【Extension Activity 2: typing】

1分間でどれだけタイプできるか計測してみましょう。

| 1st time _____ words | 2nd time _____ words |

V Integrated Skills 10

> *Name a person who influences you a lot. Describe the person and say why he/she influences you.*

CDを聴いて、(　　　　　)に記入しましょう。

　　One of the people who has been most influential in my life was my English teacher in high school. He was so strict, but (1.　　　　　) his strictness helped every student (2. 　　　　　　　　　). At the same time, he had (3. 　　　　　　). I was really inspired by his teaching and I gradually came to (4. 　　　　　　) to study abroad someday. I am now working hard to (5. 　　　　　　　) in the USA to realize my dream. (6. 　　　　　　) regarding decisions (7. 　　　　　　　　).

(97 words)

【Extension Activity 3: writing】
あなた自身の答えを書いてみましょう。

....
....
....
....
....
....
....

【Extension Activity 4: speaking】
あなた自身の答えを話してみましょう。

TOEFL® Test Skills

メモ用紙を活用しましょう。

TOEFL iBT® の解答は全てコンピュータで入力しますが、入室の際に筆記具とメモ用紙が渡されるので、活用しましょう。例えば、リスニングの講義の聞き取りでは、忘れてしまいそうな数字や大事な事柄を簡単にメモしておくと良いでしょう。英語だけでなく、矢印、簡単なイラストや漢字一字(例:経済の経だけ)、カタカナなど自分なりに工夫しましょう。

また、ライティングではメモ用紙に下書きをする時間はありませんが、自分のアイディアをまとめ、構成を考えるのにメモ用紙を使うと良いでしょう。

Unit 4　The Big Easy and Sin City

I Words and Phrases

この章で学ぶ表現を確認しましょう。

A 語群からもっとも適切な5つの語句を選びましょう。

1. 市民　　　　（　　　　　）　2. 描写する　（　　　　　）
3. 苦労して稼いだ（　　　　）　4. 賃金　　　（　　　　　）
5. 三日月形　　（　　　　　）

| describe | hard-earned | wage | citizen | crescent |

B 左側の定義にあてはまるように、空所を埋めてみましょう。

1. activity that is against the law　　（ cr _ m _ ）
2. a section of a town or city　　　　（ n _ _ _ hborhood ）
3. to finish making or doing　　　　 （ c _ mpl _ _ _ ）

II. Note-taking 🎧 11

本文を聴きながらノートをとりましょう。(英語でも日本語でも構いません)

III. Reading Aloud & Shadowing 🎧 12

CDを聴きながら、発音に気をつけて音読をしましょう。次に本を閉じて、シャドーイングしましょう。

1. Many cities have interesting nicknames.
2. Nicknames can help establish the identity of a city.
3. They can also spread pride among its citizens.
4. New Orleans, Louisiana probably has more nicknames than any other American city.

IV Reading Comprehension

Reading

❶ Many cities have interesting nicknames. Nicknames can help establish the identity of a city. They can also spread pride among its citizens. New Orleans, Louisiana probably has more nicknames than any other American city. One web site lists more than twenty nicknames. The most famous is "The Big Easy." It describes the gentle, slow and easy-going way of life in New Orleans. So how did the city get this nickname?

❷ In the early 1900s there was a dance hall in New Orleans called "The Big Easy." But the nickname did not become famous until the early 1970s. That was when a Louisiana newspaper writer began calling New Orleans by this name. She compared the easy-going way of life there to the hurried pace of life in New York City. In 1970, James Conaway wrote a crime novel called "The Big Easy." The story was set in New Orleans. In 1987, that book was made into a film which made the nickname even more popular.

❸ New Orleans has other nicknames. One of them is "The Crescent City." During the 19th century, new neighborhoods expanded out from what is now known as the French Quarter. These areas followed the great curve of the Mississippi River, giving New Orleans the shape of a crescent. Another nickname is "The Birthplace of Jazz," because that kind of music started in New Orleans. It is also called "Mardi Gras City" for the wild celebrations and parades that take place there every year. And, there is a nickname that uses the short way to write New Orleans and Louisiana. If you do not want to use the complete name, you can call the city "NOLA."

❹ One of America's most exciting cities is Las Vegas, Nevada. There you can play games of chance all night long. The city's nightclubs are also open all night for eating, drinking and dancing. So it is not surprising that Las Vegas is called "The Gambling Capital of the World" and "The Entertainment Capital of the World." Another nickname for Las Vegas is "Sin City," because you can find many kinds of adult entertainment there.

Many people who come to Las Vegas in hopes of winning lots of money do not know when to stop gambling. They may lose a great deal of their hard-earned money. So the city is also called something that sounds like Las Vegas — "Lost Wages."

(397 Words)

本文について、下記の設問に答えましょう。

1. The word **establish** in paragraph 1 is closest in meaning to
   a. create
   b. carry
   c. satisfy
   d. estimate

2. The word **They** in paragraph 1 refers to
   a. many cities
   b. nicknames
   c. New Orleans
   d. neighborhoods

3. According to paragraph 3, what is NOT TRUE about New Orleans?
   a. James Conaway directed a movie about New Orleans.
   b. Jazz music originated in New Orleans.
   c. "NOLA" stands for New Orleans, Louisiana.
   d. Mardi Gras is held in New Orleans annually.

4. What is implied about Las Vegas in paragraph 4?
   a. Las Vegas has fewer nicknames than New Orleans.
   b. A lot of activity in Las Vegas is not suitable for children.
   c. Just a few nightclubs in Las Vegas open after midnight.
   d. The most famous nickname of Las Vegas is "The Big Easy."

5. Which of the following statements is NOT true?
   a. "The Big Easy" is a nickname for New Orleans.
   b. "Sin City" is a nickname for Las Vegas.
   c. "The French Quarter" is a nickname for New Orleans.
   d. "Lost Wages" is a nickname for Las Vegas.

【Extension Activity 1: timed reading】
1分間でどれだけ読めるか計測してみましょう。

| 1st time | words | 2nd time | words |

【Extension Activity 2: typing】
1分間でどれだけタイプできるか計測してみましょう。

| 1st time | words | 2nd time | words |

V Integrated Skills 13

What are your favorite things to do on weekends?

CDを聴いて、(　　　　) に記入しましょう。

　　I usually spend the weekend in two ways. On one day, I (1.　　　　　) of the beautiful scenery in my town. Since the town (2.　　　　　), the scenery of mountains and rivers is constantly changing (3.　　　　　). I try to (4.　　　　　) recording the local environment. (5.　　　　　), I just stay at home, planning (6.　　　　　), which allows me to be ready to deal with anything. These are my favorite things to do on weekends and it helps me lead (7.　　　　　).

(101 words)

【Extension Activity 3: writing】
あなた自身の答えを書いてみましょう。

....
....
....
....
....
....

【Extension Activity 4: speaking】
あなた自身の答えを話してみましょう。

TOEFL® Test Skills

キャンパス用語クイズ （Part 2）

以下は英語圏の大学でよく使われる単語・表現です。選択肢の中からあてはまるものを選び、書きましょう。

1. 講義　　　（　　　　　） 2. 司書　　　（　　　　　）
3. 盗作・剽窃行為（　　　　　） 4. 著作権　　（　　　　　）
5. 文献目録　　（　　　　　）

librarian	bibliography
copyright	lecture
plagiarism	

Unit 5 Bigwig

1 Words and Phrases

この章で学ぶ表現を確認しましょう。

A 語群からもっとも適切な5つの語句を選びましょう。

1. 犯罪者　　（　　　　　）
2. 失敗する　（　　　　　）
3. 逮捕する　（　　　　　）
4. 取り除く　（　　　　　）
5. 活動・作戦（　　　　　）

| remove | operation | fail | criminal | arrest |

B 左側の定義にあてはまるように、空所を埋めてみましょう。

1. からかう　　　　　　　　　　　　　(make f _ _ of)
2. 喜劇役者　　　　　　　　　　　　　(com _ _ ian)
3. 〜の可能性が高い、〜しそうである　(is l _ k _ ly to)

30　TOEFL iBT® Basics

II. Note-taking 🎧 14

本文を聴きながらノートをとりましょう。(英語でも日本語でも構いません)

III. Reading Aloud & Shadowing 🎧 15

ＣＤを聴きながら、発音に気をつけて音読をしましょう。次に本を閉じて、シャドーイングしましょう。

1. In the seventeenth century, important men in Europe began to wear false hair, called wigs.
2. As years passed, wigs began to get bigger.
3. The size of a man's wig depended on how important he was.
4. The more important he was, the bigger the wig he wore.

IV Reading Comprehension

Reading

❶ Some expressions describe people who are important, or who at least think they are. (1) One such expression is bigwig. In the seventeenth century, important men in Europe began to wear false hair, called wigs. As years passed, wigs began to get bigger. (2) The size of a man's wig depended on how important he was. The more important he was — or thought he was — the bigger the wig he wore. Some wigs were so large they covered a man's shoulders or back. (3) Today, the expression bigwig is used to make fun of a person who feels important. People never tell someone he is a bigwig. (4)

❷ Big wheel is another way to describe an important person. A big wheel may be the head of a company, a political leader, a famous movie star. They are big wheels because they are powerful. What they do affects many people. Big wheels give the orders. Other people carry them out. As in many machines, a big wheel makes the little wheels turn. Big wheel became a popular expression after World War Two. It probably comes from an expression used for many years by people who fix parts of cars and trucks. They said a person rolled a big wheel if he was important and had influence.

❸ The top of something is the highest part. So it is not surprising that top is part of another expression that describes an important person. The expression is top banana. A top banana is the leading person in a comedy show. The funniest comedian is called the top banana. The next is second banana. Why a banana? A comedy act in earlier days often included a part where one of the comedians would hit the others over the head with a soft object. The object was shaped like the yellow fruit: the banana. Top banana still is used mainly in show business. Yet the expression can also be used to describe the top person in any area.

❹ A kingpin is another word for an important person. The expression comes from the game of bowling. The kingpin is the number one pin. If hit correctly with the bowling ball, the kingpin will make all the other nine pins fall. And that is the object of the game. So, the most important person in a project or business is the kingpin. If the kingpin is removed, the business or project is likely to fail. Kingpin is often used to describe an important criminal, or the leader of a criminal gang. A newspaper may report, for example, that police have arrested the suspected kingpin of a car-stealing operation.

(440 Words)

本文について、下記の設問に答えましょう。

1. The word **fix** in paragraph 2 is closest in meaning to
   a. attach
   b. repair
   c. pick
   d. cook

2. The word **suspected** in paragraph 4 is closest in meaning to
   a. expected
   b. dangerous
   c. suspicious
   d. imaginary

3. Look at the four numbers that indicate where the following sentence could be added to paragraph 1.

   They only use the expression behind his back.

   Where would the sentence best fit?
   a. (1)
   b. (2)
   c. (3)
   d. (4)

4. According to paragraph 3, all of the following statements are true EXCEPT
   a. The phrase "top banana" is only used in show business.
   b. In a comedy show, the leading person is the "top banana."
   c. Comedians used to hit each other with an object that looked like a banana.
   d. "Top banana" refers to the funniest comedian.

5. The expressions in the article are related to all of the following EXCEPT
   a. bowling
   b. musicians
   c. show business
   d. criminals

【Extension Activity 1: timed reading】
1分間でどれだけ読めるか計測してみましょう。

| 1st time   words | 2nd time   words |

【Extension Activity 2: typing】
1分間でどれだけタイプできるか計測してみましょう。

| 1st time   words | 2nd time   words |

V Integrated Skills

Name a place in your country you would recommend others to visit.

CDを聴いて、(   ) に記入しましょう。

Kyoto is famous for (1.   ), which remind people of (2.   ). People coming to Kyoto often say that (3.   ) and at home in this historical city. However, this city has (4.   ): it is always creating new things. For example, new shops and restaurants (5.   ) and people in Kyoto are always trying to create new food, products, and entertainment (6.   ). When you visit Kyoto, try to find the two sides of the city: (7.   ).

(89 words)

【Extension Activity 3: writing】
あなた自身の答えを書いてみましょう。

::
::
::
::
::
::

【Extension Activity 4: speaking】
あなた自身の答えを話してみましょう。

TOEFL® Test Skills

TOEFL iBT® Reading 攻略法（時間配分）

制限時間60〜80分で、アカデミックな文章の抜粋、3または4パッセージを読み、39〜56問の問題に答えます。（なお、リーディングとリスニングには、採点されない追加設問が含まれる場合もあります。）

1つのパッセージごとに、読んでかつ設問に答えるのに20分の時間制限があります。画面上に時計が出て残り時間を示します。

設問には内容把握の問題に加えて、必ず2〜3問の同義語または反意語を問う問題、1つのパラグラフの中で抜けている文をどこか適切な場所に挿入する問題、最後に全体の要約を完成するのに必要な文を選ぶ問題（2点分）が出ます。時間配分を考えて解答する練習をしましょう。

Unit 6 Grapevine

I Words and Phrases

この章で学ぶ表現を確認しましょう。

A 語群からもっとも適切な5つの語句を選びましょう。

1. 遠いかなたの　（　　　　　）　2. 実験する　（　　　　　）
3. ほめたたえる　（　　　　　）　4. 電報　（　　　　　）
5. 司令官　（　　　　　）

| telegraph | far-off | commander | experiment | honor |

B 接頭辞をつけて反対語にしましょう。

［例］comfortable　⇔　(uncomfortable)

1. responsible　⇔　（　　　　　）
2. appear　　　⇔　（　　　　　）
3. complete　　⇔　（　　　　　）

II. Note-taking 🎧 17

本文を聴きながらノートをとりましょう。（英語でも日本語でも構いません）

III. Reading Aloud & Shadowing 🎧 18

ＣＤを聴きながら、発音に気をつけて音読をしましょう。次に本を閉じて、シャドーイングしましょう。

1. The expression "by the grapevine" is more than one hundred years old.
2. The American inventor, Samuel F. Morse, is largely responsible for the birth of the expression.
3. Among others, he experimented with the idea of telegraphy.
4. When Morse finally completed his telegraphic instrument, he went before Congress to show that it worked.

IV. Reading Comprehension

Reading

❶ Some of the most exciting information comes by way of the grapevine. That is so because reports received through the grapevine are supposed to be secret. The information is all hush hush. It is whispered into your ear with the understanding that you will not pass it on to others. You feel honored and excited. You are one of the special few to get this information. You cannot wait. You must quickly find other ears to pour the information into. And so, the information — secret as it is — begins to spread. Nobody knows how far.

❷ The expression by the grapevine is more than one hundred years old. The American inventor, Samuel F. Morse, is largely responsible for the birth of the expression. Among others, he experimented with the idea of telegraphy — sending messages over a wire by electricity. When Morse finally completed his telegraphic instrument, he went before Congress to show that it worked. He sent a message over a wire from Washington to Baltimore. The message was: "What hath God wrought?" This was on May twenty-fourth, eighteen forty-four.

❸ Quickly, companies began to build telegraph lines from one place to another. Men everywhere seemed to be putting up poles with strings of wire for carrying telegraphic messages. The workmanship was poor. And the wires were not put up straight. Some of the results looked strange. People said they looked like a grapevine. A large number of the telegraph lines were going in all directions, as crooked as the vines that grapes grow on. So was born the expression, by the grapevine.

❹ Some writers believe that the phrase would soon have disappeared were it not for the American Civil War. Soon after the war began in eighteen sixty-one, military commanders started to send battlefield reports by telegraph. People began hearing the phrase by the grapevine to describe false as well as true reports from the battlefield. It was like a game. Was it true? Who says so?

⑤ Now, as in those far-off Civil War days, getting information by the grapevine remains something of a game. A friend brings you a bit of strange news. "No," you say, "it just can't be true! Who told you?" Comes the answer, "I got it by the grapevine." You really cannot know how much — if any — of the information that comes to you by the grapevine is true or false. Still, in the words of an old American saying, the person who keeps pulling the grapevine shakes down at least a few grapes.

(418 Words)

本文について、下記の設問に答えましょう。

1. The expression **hush hush** in paragraph 1 is closest in meaning to
   a. patchwork   **b.** hasty
   c. jumble   **d.** confidential

2. The word **inventor** in paragraph 2 refers to
   a. invader   **b.** innovator
   c. artisan   **d.** incubator

3. In paragraph 3, the author says that early telegraph lines were
   a. built in a straight line   **b.** not well built
   c. held up by string   **d.** held up by wire

4. In paragraph 4, the author states all of the following EXCEPT
   a. The phrase "by the grapevine" disappeared during the American Civil War.
   b. During the American Civil War, messages were sent using the telegraph.
   c. You could hear true reports by the grapevine.
   d. You could hear false reports by the grapevine.

5. According to the article, the following are all correct EXCEPT

   a. Morse was the first man to use the expression, by the grapevine.
   b. You are not supposed to share what you hear by the grapevine.
   c. It's impossible to know whether information by the grapevine is correct or not.
   d. The expression began because telegraph lines were not straight, and looked like crooked grapevines.

【Extension Activity 1: timed reading】
1分間でどれだけ読めるか計測してみましょう。

| 1st time   words | 2nd time   words |

【Extension Activity 2: typing】
1分間でどれだけタイプできるか計測してみましょう。

| 1st time   words | 2nd time   words |

V Integrated Skills   19

Where would you like to go to spend a vacation? Describe this place and say why you would like to have a holiday there.

CD を聴いて、(   ) に記入しましょう。

If I could (1.   ) in the summer, I would like to go to the United Kingdom and travel around the country. The UK (2.   ): England, Scotland, Wales, and Northern Ireland, each of which has (3.   ). I would like to visit each country and try (4.   ). In addition, visiting such tourist sites as castles or the birthplaces of famous writers and artists would educate me (5.   ). Through the vacation, I would hope to (6.   ) to the UK and surely enjoy (7.   ) experience.

(104 words)

40   TOEFL iBT® Basics

【Extension Activity 3: writing】
あなた自身の答えを書いてみましょう。

....
....
....
....
....
....

【Extension Activity 4: speaking】
あなた自身の答えを話してみましょう。

TOEFL® Test Skills

TOEFL iBT® Listening 攻略

TOEFL iBT® のリスニングでは制限時間 60 〜 90 分で、講義、授業中の討論、学生や教職員の会話を聴いた後に、34 〜 51 問の問題に答えます。（なお、リーディング同様、リスニングには、採点されない追加設問が含まれる場合もあります。）

なお、米国、カナダのアクセントだけでなく、英国、ニュージーランド、オーストラリアといった地域のネイティブスピーカーによる英語のアクセントも含まれています。普段から海外のドキュメンタリー番組やニュースを英語音声で聴き、自然なスピードの英語に慣れておくと良いでしょう。

Unit 7 Quit Buggin' Me!

1 Words and Phrases

この章で学ぶ表現を確認しましょう。

A 語群からもっとも適切な5つの語句を選びましょう。

1. 蟻　　　　　(　　　　)　2. スズメバチ　(　　　　)
3. ナンキンムシ (　　　　)　4. ミツバチの巣 (　　　　)
5. ひざ　　　　(　　　　)

> hive　　bedbug　　knee　　ant　　hornet

B 左側の単語とほぼ同じ意味を示す表現を選びましょう。

1. motionless　　　(　　　　)
2. immediately　　(　　　　)
3. scramble　　　　(　　　　)

> stir up　　sitting still　　right away

II. Note-taking 🎧20

本文を聴きながらノートをとりましょう。(英語でも日本語でも構いません)

III. Reading Aloud & Shadowing 🎧21

ＣＤを聴きながら、発音に気をつけて音読をしましょう。次に本を閉じて、シャドーイングしましょう。

1. Here is an expression about bees that is not used much anymore, but we like it anyway.

2. If something was the best of its kind, you might say it was "the bee's knees."

3. If someone asks you a personal question, you might say "That is none of your beeswax."

4. This means "none of your business."

IV. Reading Comprehension

① There are many American expressions about insects — like bees, for example. Bees are known as very hard workers. They always appear to be busy, moving around their homes, or hives. So you might say you were "as busy as a bee" if you spent your weekend cleaning your house. In fact, you might say your house was "a beehive of activity", if your whole family was helping you clean. You also might say you "made a beeline" for something if you went there right away. When we go to see a movie, my friend always "makes a beeline" for the place where they sell popcorn.

② Here is an expression about bees that is not used much anymore, but we like it anyway. We think it was first used in the 1920s. If something was the best of its kind, you might say it was "the bee's knees." Now, we admit that we do not know how this expression developed — in fact, we do not even know if bees have knees! If your friend cannot stop talking about something because she thinks it is important, you might say she has "a bee in her bonnet." If someone asks you a personal question, you might say "That is none of your beeswax." This means "none of your business."

③ Speaking of personal questions, there is an expression people sometimes use when their children ask, "Where do babies come from?" Parents who discuss sex and reproduction say this is talking about "the birds and the bees." Hornets are bee-like insects that sometimes attack people. If you are really angry, you might say you are "mad as a hornet." And if you "stir up a hornet's nest," you create trouble or problems.

④ Butterflies are beautiful insects, but you would not want to have "butterflies in your stomach." That means to be nervous about having to do something, like speaking in front of a crowd. You would also not want to have "ants in your pants" — that is, to be restless and unable to sit still.

⑤ Here are some expressions about plain old bugs — another word for insects. If a friend keeps asking you to do something you do not want to do, you might ask him to leave you alone or "stop bugging me." A friend also might tell you again and again to do something. If so, you might say he "put a bug in your ear." If you were reading a book in your warm bed on a cold winter's day, you might say you were "snug as a bug in a rug." And, if you wish someone good night, you might say, "Sleep tight — don't let the bedbugs bite."

(452 Words)

本文について、下記の設問に答えましょう。

1. The word **reproduction** in paragraph 3 is closest in meaning to
   a. imitation
   b. breeding
   c. subtraction
   d. replica

2. The word **nervous** in paragraph 4 refers to
   a. gullible
   b. extroverted
   c. naive
   d. tense

3. Paragraph 3 introduces the phrase, "Stir up a hornet's nest." What does this mean?
   a. get really angry
   b. attack many people
   c. make a difficult situation
   d. go crazy

4. According to paragraph 5, what does it mean if someone says to you, "Stop bugging me"?
   a. "Please tell me again and again."
   b. "Don't try to help me."
   c. "Don't bother me."
   d. "Get these bugs off me."

5. If something is really good, how do you describe it?

   a. the bee's knees
   b. the birds and the bees
   c. a bee in your bonnet
   d. beeswax

【Extension Activity 1: timed reading】
1分間でどれだけ読めるか計測してみましょう。

| 1st time | words | | 2nd time | words |

【Extension Activity 2: typing】
1分間でどれだけタイプできるか計測してみましょう。

| 1st time | words | | 2nd time | words |

V Integrated Skills 🎧 22

> Some people think it is a good idea for university students to have part-time jobs. Do you agree or disagree?

CDを聴いて、(   )に記入しましょう。

　People engage in (1.   ) in their lifetime. (2.   ), university students should have the opportunity to do some part-time work before they (3.   ). Through working in any job, they can learn (4.   ) that they cannot learn at university. For instance, students who work in a restaurant learn how to (5.   ), as well as how to serve and satisfy customers. Such experience and skills acquired through a part-time job help (6.   ), and are of great help (7.   ).

(95 words)

【Extension Activity 3: writing】
あなた自身の答えを書いてみましょう。

....
....
....
....
....
....
....

【Extension Activity 4: speaking】
あなた自身の答えを話してみましょう。

TOEFL® Test Skills

自然科学用語クイズ

以下は自然科学の分野でよく使用される用語です。英語の定義にあう適切な単語を下の語群より選び、( )内に書き入れてみましょう。

| mammal habitat respiration bacteria nourishment |

(   ): the process of breathing
(   ): the natural home of a plant or animal
(   ): the food necessary for growth, health, and good condition
(   ): very small living things, some of which cause illness or disease
(   ): a type of animal that drinks milk from its mother's body when it is young

Unit 8 It's Not Worth a Hill of Beans!

1 Words and Phrases

この章で学ぶ表現を確認しましょう。

A 語群からもっとも適切な5つの語句を選びましょう。

1. 賭け金　（　　　　　）　　2. 農業の　（　　　　　）
3. 条件　　（　　　　　）　　4. 家賃　　（　　　　　）
5. 穀物　　（　　　　　）

> rent　　grain　　bet　　condition　　agricultural

B 左側の定義にあてはまるように、空所を埋めてみましょう。

1. ～と関係がある　　　（ is l_nked to ）
2. 用心のために　　　　（ to be on the s_fe side ）
3. 昼日中に　　　　　　（ in the mi_dle of the day ）

48　TOEFL iBT® Basics

II Note-taking 🎧 23

本文を聴きながらノートをとりましょう。（英語でも日本語でも構いません）

III Reading Aloud & Shadowing 🎧 24

ＣＤを聴きながら、発音に気をつけて音読をしましょう。次に本を閉じて、シャドーイングしましょう。

1. Since the 16th century, the word "farm" has meant agricultural land.
2. But a much older meaning of the word "farm" is linked to economics.
3. The word "farm" comes from the Latin word "firma."
4. The earliest meaning of the English word "farm" was a yearly payment made as a tax or rent.

IV Reading Comprehension

Reading

①   In the early days of human history, people survived by hunting wild animals or gathering wild grains and plants for food. Then, some people learned to grow crops and raise animals for food. They were the first farmers. Since the 16th century, the word "farm" has meant agricultural land. But a much older meaning of the word "farm" is linked to economics. The word "farm" comes from the Latin word "firma," which means an unchanging payment. Experts say the earliest meaning of the English word "farm" was a yearly payment made as a tax or rent. Farmers in early England did not own their land — they paid every year to use agricultural lands.

②   In England, farmers used hawthorn trees along the edges of property. They called this row of hawthorns a "hedge." Hedging fields was how careful farmers marked and protected them. Soon, people began to use the word "hedging" to describe steps that could be taken to protect against financial loss. Hedging is common among gamblers who make large bets. A gambler bets a lot of money on one team. But, to be on the safe side, he also places a smaller bet on the other team to reduce a possible loss. You might say that someone is "hedging his bet" when he invests in several different kinds of businesses. One business may fail, but likely not all.

③   Farmers know that it is necessary to "make hay while the sun shines." Hay has to be cut and gathered when it is dry. So a wise farmer never postpones gathering his hay when the sun is shining — rain may soon appear. A wise person copies the farmer. He works when conditions are right. A new mother, for example, quickly learns to try to sleep when her baby is quiet — even in the middle of the day. If the mother delays, she may lose her chance to sleep. So, the mother learns to "make hay while the sun shines."

④   Beans are a popular farm crop. But beans are used to describe something of very little value in the expression "not worth a hill of beans." The expression is often used today. You could say, for example, that a bad idea "is not worth a hill of beans." Language expert Charles Earle Funk said the expression was first used almost 700 years ago. He said Robert of Gloucester described a message from the King of Germany to King John of England as "altogether not worth a bean."

(415 Words)

本文について、下記の設問に答えましょう。

1. The word **raise** in paragraph 1 is closest in meaning to
   a. reinforce
   b. hoist
   c. grow
   d. provoke

2. The word **property** in paragraph 2 is closest in meaning to
   a. acquisition
   b. estate
   c. equity
   d. backing

3. According to paragraph 1, all of the following are true EXCEPT
   a. The word "farm" was originally a Latin word.
   b. The word "farm" has its origins in economics.
   c. Farm used to be a kind of tax that farmers paid.
   d. In England, a long time ago, most farmers owned their land.

4. In paragraph 3, how is "make hay while the sun shines" explained?
   a. to work when you have the chance
   b. to sleep all the time
   c. to hate working in the rain
   d. to postpone working

5. What type of people are NOT mentioned in the article?

   a. gamblers   **b.** businessmen

   c. mothers   **d.** farmers

【Extension Activity 1: timed reading】
1分間でどれだけ読めるか計測してみましょう。

1st time	words	2nd time	words

【Extension Activity 2: typing】
1分間でどれだけタイプできるか計測してみましょう。

1st time	words	2nd time	words

V Integrated Skills 🎧 25

> *Some people believe that being on the Internet is a better way to spend time than reading books. Which do you prefer and why?*

CDを聴いて、(　　　　　)に記入しましょう。

    I don't think that being on the Internet is a better way to spend time than reading books. (¹.　　　　　), it is not appropriate to directly (².　　　　　) because the purpose of using the Internet is different from (³.　　　　　). I use the Internet to (⁴.　　　　　), to find necessary information or to (⁵.　　　　　). On the other hand, I read books (⁶.　　　　　) and to refresh myself. Both the Internet and books are (⁷.　　　　　) for different reasons.

(91 words)

【Extension Activity 3: writing】
あなた自身の答えを書いてみましょう。

．．．
．．．
．．．
．．．
．．．
．．．

【Extension Activity 4: speaking】
あなた自身の答えを話してみましょう。

TOEFL® Test Skills

TOEFL iBT® Speaking 攻略

TOEFL iBT® の Speaking セクションの形式に慣れましょう。

"Independent tasks"（スピーキングのみのタスク）（問題数 2 問、準備時間 15 秒・解答時間 45 秒）

"Integrated tasks"（複数の技能のタスク）問題数 4 問。内訳は以下のとおり。

    Reading & Listening & Speaking
        問題数 2 問、準備時間 30 秒・解答時間 60 秒

    Listening & Speaking
        問題数 2 問、準備時間 20 秒・解答時間 60 秒

音読やシャドーイングの練習をし、普段から「声を出す」練習をしましょう。次に、タイマーを使って、"Independent tasks" の練習から始めてみると良いでしょう。公式ホームページなどのトピックを参考に、実際の試験を想定して、スマートフォンなどで自分のスピーチを録音して、練習しましょう。

Unit 9 What's a GI Joe?

I Words and Phrases

この章で学ぶ表現を確認しましょう。

A 語群からもっとも適切な5つの語句を選びましょう。

1. 海兵隊　　（　　　　　）　2. 連合国　　　　（　　　　　　　）
3. 進軍する　（　　　　　）　4. 亜鉛メッキ鉄板（　　　　　　　）
5. 部隊　　　（　　　　　）

| the Allies | galvanized iron | troop | Marines | march |

B 左側の単語を名詞形に変えましょう。

［例］describe　→　(description)

1. publish　→　(　　　　　　　)
2. strong　　→　(　　　　　　　)
3. distant　 →　(　　　　　　　)

II. Note-taking 🎧 26

本文を聴きながらノートをとりましょう。（英語でも日本語でも構いません）

III. Reading Aloud & Shadowing 🎧 27

ＣＤを聴きながら、発音に気をつけて音読をしましょう。次に本を閉じて、シャドーイングしましょう。

1. Today, a doughboy or GI may be called a "grunt."
2. Nobody is sure of the exact beginning of the word.
3. A member of the United States Marines also has a strange name: "leatherneck."
4. It is thought to have started in the 1800s.

IV. Reading Comprehension

Reading

❶ A "leatherneck" or a "grunt" do not sound like nice names to call someone. Yet men and women who serve in the United States armed forces are proud of those names. And if you think they sound strange, consider "doughboy" and "GI Joe." After the American Civil War in the 1860s, a writer in a publication called *Beadle's Monthly* used the word "doughboy" to describe Civil War soldiers. But word expert Charles Funk says that early writers could not explain where the name started.

❷ About twenty years later, someone *did* explain. She was the wife of the famous American general George Custer. Elizabeth Custer wrote that a "doughboy" was a sweet food served to Navy men on ships. She also said the name was given to the large buttons on the clothes of soldiers. Elizabeth Custer believed the name changed over time to mean the soldiers themselves.

❸ Now, we probably most often think of "doughboys" as the soldiers who fought for the Allies in World War I. By World War II, soldiers were called other names. The one most often heard was "GI," or "GI Joe." Most people say the letters GI were a short way to say "general issue" or "government issue." The name came to mean several things: It could mean the soldier himself. It could mean things given to soldiers when they joined the military such as weapons, equipment or clothes. And, for some reason, it could mean to organize, or clean. Soldiers often say, "We GI'd the place." And when an area looks good, soldiers may say the area is "GI." Strangely, though, "GI" can also mean poor work, a job badly done.

❹ Some students of military words have another explanation of "GI." They say that instead of "government issue" or "general issue," "GI" came from the words "galvanized iron." The American soldier was said to be like galvanized iron — a material produced for special strength. The *Dictionary of Soldier Talk* says "GI" was used for the words "galvanized iron" in a publication about the vehicles of the early 20th century.

❺ Today, a doughboy or GI may be called a "grunt." Nobody is sure of the exact beginning of the word. But the best idea probably is that the name comes from the sound that troops make when ordered to march long distances carrying heavy equipment. A member of the United States Marines also has a strange name: "leatherneck." It is thought to have started in the 1800s. Some say the name comes from the thick collars of leather early Marines wore around their necks to protect them from cuts during battles. Others say the sun burned the Marines' necks until their skin looked like leather.

(449 Words)

本文について、下記の設問に答えましょう。

1. The word **served** in paragraph 2 is closest in meaning to

   a. employed   **b.** worked
   c. determined   **d.** offered

2. The word **several** in paragraph 3 refers to

   a. individual   **b.** common
   c. plural   **d.** specific

3. According to paragraph 3, "GI" could mean any of the following EXCEPT

   a. a well-performed job   **b.** military equipment
   c. a soldier   **d.** cleaning

4. Which of the following is TRUE according to paragraph 5?

   a. We now know for sure how the expression "grunt" began.
   b. The word "leatherneck" is about 300 years old.
   c. The leather collars often cut into soldiers' necks.
   d. Troops marching long distances made "grunt" sounds.

5. Look at the four options below and decide which one best summarizes the article. Incorrect answers either leave out or misrepresent essential information.

   a. A lot of expressions that refer to soldiers are negative, which is why they change so much over the years.
   b. There are a variety of informal words and phrases to refer to the military. The origins of some are known, but for others the roots are less clear.
   c. The wife of George Custer was an expert on military language, and she was responsible for many of the words used to describe soldiers.
   d. Using slang words to talk about troops is wrong, which is why it's better to just refer to them as "soldiers."

【Extension Activity 1: timed reading】
1分間でどれだけ読めるか計測してみましょう。

| 1st time   words | 2nd time   words |

【Extension Activity 2: typing】
1分間でどれだけタイプできるか計測してみましょう。

| 1st time   words | 2nd time   words |

V Integrated Skills 🎧 28

Which do you prefer, working on your assignments alone, or in a group?

CDを聴いて、(   )に記入しましょう。

People have (1.   ). When I work on an assignment, I prefer to study in a group. There are (2.   ) to this. Working with a group, we can (3.   ), which helps us broaden our knowledge. Moreover, we can learn how to interact with each other by realizing that everyone has (4.   ). That is, group work gives us opportunities for (5.   ). That is why I choose to (6.   ) and why I think it will bring us (7.   ) than studying alone.   (93 words)

58 TOEFL iBT® Basics

【Extension Activity 3: writing】
あなた自身の答えを書いてみましょう。

....
....
....
....
....
....
....

【Extension Activity 4: speaking】
あなた自身の答えを話してみましょう。

TOEFL® Test Skills

TOEFL iBT® Writing 攻略

TOEFL iBT® では、ライティングが最後に実施され、2種類の問題（Integrated Task と Independent Task）について、50分以内で、コンピュータを使用してライティングをします。

Integrated Task
読んだり聞いたりした内容を基にエッセイ形式の答案を書く問題（自分の意見は求められない）ワード数の目安：150〜225ワード程度

Independent Task
与えられたトピックについて自分の意見を書く問題　ワード数の目安：300ワード

日頃から英文を書くことに慣れていないとすぐには書けません。毎日英語で日記などを書くのも良い練習になります。また標準の英語 keyboard（QWERTY クォーティー配列）を使用するので、タイプ練習する時には気をつけましょう。

Unit 10 Great Scott

Words and Phrases

この章で学ぶ表現を確認しましょう。

A 語群からもっとも適切な5つの語句を選びましょう。

1. 大統領職　　（　　　　　）　2. 指名　　（　　　　　）
3. 選挙活動　　（　　　　　）　4. 対抗者　（　　　　　）
5. 候補者　　　（　　　　　）

> candidate　　opponent　　campaign　　nomination　　presidency

B 左側の定義にあてはまるように、空所を埋めてみましょう。

1. 南北戦争　　　　（ C _ _ _ _ War ）
2. 宗教的な　　　　（ r _ _ _ gious ）
3. 占拠する　　　　（ o _ _ _ py ）

II. Note-taking 🎧 29

本文を聴きながらノートをとりましょう。（英語でも日本語でも構いません）

III. Reading Aloud & Shadowing 🎧 30

ＣＤを聴きながら、発音に気をつけて音読をしましょう。次に本を閉じて、シャドーイングしましょう。

1. Every language has its ways of expressing strong emotions.
2. At times, only very mild expressions are socially accepted.
3. Some of the most popular expressions are those that are guaranteed not to offend anyone.
4. Most of these exclamations have survived from earlier days.

IV Reading Comprehension

Reading

① Every language has its ways of expressing strong emotions — surprise, shock, anger. The expressions range from mild to strong, from exclamations and oaths, to curses and swear words. The ones that are accepted in public speech change through the years as social rules change.

② At times, only very mild expressions are socially accepted. Some of the most popular expressions are those that are guaranteed not to offend anyone. Most of these exclamations have survived from earlier days. And their original meanings are long since forgotten.

③ Great Scott! is a good example. It expresses surprise or shock. You might say to someone, "Great Scott! I did not know she was married!" (1) Language expert Webb Garrison tells an interesting story about the expression. Just before the Civil War, the Whig political party was making a last effort to remain a part of American political life. (2) They thought that Winfield Scott would be the right candidate. In his thirty years as a general, Winfield Scott had become one of the best-known military leaders in the country. (3) During the war with Mexico, he had captured Vera Cruz and occupied Mexico City. So, party leaders thought that if any Whig could be elected president, it was Winfield Scott. (4)

④ General Scott quickly accepted the nomination and began campaigning. It did not take long for the public to realize that General Scott really liked General Scott! His speeches were full of praise for himself. It was evident that he thought he was the greatest candidate who had ever lived. Soon his political opponents began to make fun of him. They called him, Great Scott. General Scott did not come close to winning the presidency. But his name still lives as part of the English language.

⑤ Other popular exclamations combine holy with other words. Holy Mackerel! is one that expresses surprise or wonder. It comes from earlier days when the Roman Catholic Church ruled that Catholics must not eat meat on Fridays. Since mackerel was a common and cheap fish in the United States, it was often eaten for dinner on Friday. Then there is Holy Toledo! It is another expression of surprise. It refers to the city of Toledo, Spain, an important religious center in medieval times. Toledo was a holy city for both the Roman Catholics and the Muslim Moors of Spain.

(390 Words)

本文について、下記の設問に答えましょう。

1. The word **praise** in paragraph 4 is closest in meaning to
   a. compliment
   b. concentration
   c. overwhelming
   d. amazement

2. The word **medieval** in paragraph 5 refers to
   a. current
   b. affirmative
   c. historic
   d. feudal

3. Look at the four numbers that indicate where the following sentence could be added to paragraph 3.

   For the election of 1852, the Whigs wanted to offer a colorful candidate for president.

   Where would the sentence best fit?
   a. (1)   b. (2)   c. (3)   d. (4)

4. According to paragraph 5, why did Catholics use to eat mackerel on Fridays?
   a. It was tastier than meat.
   b. Catholics were not allowed to eat meat on Fridays.
   c. Meat was too expensive.
   d. It was a holy fish.

5. Look at the four options below and decide which one best summarizes the article. Incorrect answers either leave out or misrepresent essential information.

   a. General Winfield Scott was a very proud man, and he had a high opinion of himself. For this reason, the expression "Great Scott" was coined.
   b. Many expressions have religious origins, but they are only used by Catholics and Muslims.
   c. You must be very careful when using expressions of shock, surprise, or anger, because even if an expression was acceptable in the past, it might be very rude today.
   d. There are many expressions to express surprise, shock and anger, some socially acceptable and some not. Expressions may have political or religious origins.

【Extension Activity 1: timed reading】
1分間でどれだけ読めるか計測してみましょう。

| 1st time | words | 2nd time | words |

【Extension Activity 2: typing】
1分間でどれだけタイプできるか計測してみましょう。

| 1st time | words | 2nd time | words |

V Integrated Skills   31

Do you prefer to spend your free time on indoor or outdoor activities?

CDを聴いて、(   )に記入しましょう。

I prefer to spend my free time (1.   ) because I don't like going outside to do (2.   ) such as camping, mountain climbing, or jogging. (3.   ), I don't want to be bothered by (4.   ), either. When I have free time, I usually stay at home relaxing in order to (5.   ). By doing so, I can (6.   ) to work hard. I would like to spend my free time doing (7.   ), so that I can be refreshed.

(89 words)

【Extension Activity 3: writing】
あなた自身の答えを書いてみましょう。

....
....
....
....
....
....

【Extension Activity 4: speaking】
あなた自身の答えを話してみましょう。

TOEFL® Test Skills

語彙力強化のために

TOEFL iBT® のリーディングでは語彙問題、パラグラフごとの内容理解問題、全体の要旨把握問題などが出題されます。普段から 1. 英英辞典を使用する。2. アカデミックな語彙を増やす。3. 長文を速読する力を身につける。4. 英字新聞や洋書を読み、多読の習慣を身につける、といったことを心がけましょう。

TOEFL iBT® テストで出題される語彙は、アカデミックな内容に関連しているため、さまざまな分野の背景知識や専門用語を知っておく必要があります。わからない単語の意味を調べる場合、英和辞典を使用すると日本語で意味を確認することができますが、日本語の意味は必ずしも英単語と同じ意味をカバーしているとは言えません。

例えば、英語の "career" とはどんな意味でしょうか。ロングマン現代英英辞典によると "a job or profession that you have been trained for, and which you do for a long period of your life" であり、生涯の長期にわたって就く仕事（専門職）であることがわかりますね。英英辞典を使うことで、単語の意味、用法がわかるだけでなく、英文を読むことでリーディングの訓練にもなります。継続して取り組みましょう。

Unit 11 Swan Song

❶ Words and Phrases

この章で学ぶ表現を確認しましょう。

A 語群からもっとも適切な5つの語句を選びましょう。

1. 市長　　　（　　　　　）　　2. 詩人　　（　　　　　）
3. 哲学者　　（　　　　　）　　4. 投票　　（　　　　　）
5. 副大統領　（　　　　　）

| vice president | mayor | philosopher | vote | poet |

B [ ] 内の文字を並べ替えて、左側の単語と同意の英単語にしてみましょう。

1. 優雅な　　　　　　　　　　　g[ucraef]l　　＿＿＿＿＿＿＿＿
2. 候補者　　　　　　　　　　　c[naadidt]e　　＿＿＿＿＿＿＿＿
3. 〜の後を継ぐ、〜に取って変わる　r[aelpc]e　　＿＿＿＿＿＿＿＿

II. Note-taking 🎧 32

本文を聴きながらノートをとりましょう。（英語でも日本語でも構いません）

III. Reading Aloud & Shadowing 🎧 33

CDを聴きながら、発音に気をつけて音読をしましょう。次に本を閉じて、シャドーイングしましょう。

1. The swan is mostly silent through its life.
2. It floats quietly on the water, unable to sing sweet songs like most other birds.
3. In ancient times, however, people believed that the swan was given a special gift of song at the end of its life.
4. They believed a swan sings a most beautiful song just before it dies.

IV Reading Comprehension

Reading

❶ The white swan — with its long, graceful neck — is among the most beautiful of birds. The swan is mostly silent through its life. It floats quietly on the water, unable to sing sweet songs like most other birds. In ancient times, however, people believed that the swan was given a special gift of song at the end of its life. They believed a swan sings a most beautiful song just before it dies. The ancient Greek philosopher Socrates talked of this two thousand three hundred years ago. Socrates explained that the swan was singing because it was happy. The bird was happy because it was going to serve the Greek God Apollo. Swans were holy to Apollo, the god of poetry and song.

❷ The story of the swan's last song found a place in the works of other writers, including the early English writers Chaucer and Shakespeare. And, the expression swan song has long been a part of the English language. At first, swan song meant the last work of a poet, musician or writer. Now, it means the final effort of any person. Someone's swan song usually is also considered that person's finest work.

❸ A political expression with a similar meaning is **the last hurrah**. The expression may be used to describe a politician's last campaign, his final attempt to win the cheers and votes of the people. The last hurrah also can mean the last acts of a politician, before his term in office ends. Writer Edwin O'Connor made the expression popular in nineteen fifty-six. He wrote a book about the final years in the political life of a long-time mayor of Boston, Massachusetts. He called his book, *The Last Hurrah*.

❹ (1) Some language experts say the expression came from a name given to noisy supporters of Andrew Jackson…America's seventh president. They cheered **hurrah** so loudly for Andy Jackson during his presidential campaign that they became known as the **hurrah boys**. (2) Jackson's hurrah boys also played a part in the election to choose the next president.

Jackson's choice was his vice president, Martin Van Buren. (3) A newspaper of the time reported that Van Buren was elected president, in its words: "...by the hurrah boys, and those who knew just enough to shout hurrah for Jackson." (4)

(380 Words)

本文について、下記の設問に答えましょう。

1. The word **effort** in paragraph 2 is closest in meaning to

   a. endeavor
   b. destruction
   c. commencement
   d. indication

2. The word **term** in paragraph 3 is closest in meaning to

   a. incumbency
   b. nomenclature
   c. semester
   d. indication

3. According to paragraph 1, which of the following statements is TRUE?

   a. Swans sing throughout their lives.
   b. Long ago, people believed swans sang just before their own death.
   c. The Greek philosopher Socrates didn't believe that swans could sing.
   d. The Greek God Apollo had no need for swans.

4. Look at the four numbers that indicate where the following sentence could be added to paragraph 4.

   So, President Jackson really heard his last hurrahs in the campaign of another candidate, the man who would replace him in the White House.

   Where would the sentence best fit?

   a. (1)   b. (2)   c. (3)   d. (4)

5. All of the following are mentioned in the article EXCEPT

　a. famous writers　　　**b.** an ancient philosopher
　c. a popular singer　　**d.** a president of the USA

【Extension Activity 1: timed reading】
１分間でどれだけ読めるか計測してみましょう。

| 1st time | words | 2nd time | words |

【Extension Activity 2: typing】
１分間でどれだけタイプできるか計測してみましょう。

| 1st time | words | 2nd time | words |

V Integrated Skills　34

Do you prefer long vacations or short vacations? Why?

CD を聴いて、(　　　　) に記入しましょう。

　　I prefer long vacations to short vacations for (1.　　　　　).
First, we can (2.　　　　　) of tourism if we plan to take a trip during a long vacation. In a long vacation, we can (3.　　　　　) and high prices as we (4.　　　　　) of the dates to travel. Second, if the vacation time is longer, we can take a long trip even (5.　　　　　). Finally, we can spend more time relaxing (6.　　　　　) by study, work, or (7.　　　　　).
(85 words)

【Extension Activity 3: writing】
あなた自身の答えを書いてみましょう。

....
....
....
....
....
....
....

【Extension Activity 4: speaking】
あなた自身の答えを話してみましょう。

TOEFL® Test Skills

地理・歴史用語クイズ

以下は地理・歴史の分野でよく使用される用語です。英語の定義にあう適切な単語を選び、〇で囲みましょう。

1. a narrow passage of water between two areas of land, usually connecting two seas
   [arctic   strait   equator   latitude]

2. someone who enters another country to live there permanently
   [colony   citizen   delegate   immigrant]

3. an important official statement about a particular situation or plan, or the act of making this statement
   [revolution   exploration   declaration   representation]

Unit 12　When Is a Choice Not Really a Choice?

I Words and Phrases

この章で学ぶ表現を確認しましょう。

A 語群からもっとも適切な5つの語句を選びましょう。

1. 残業する　（　　　　　）　　2. 修理する　（　　　　　）
3. 溺れる　　（　　　　　）　　4. 割れ目　　（　　　　　）
5. 馬小屋　　（　　　　　）

| fix | stable | drown | crack | work late |

B 左側の反対語を書いてみましょう。

1. subordinate　⇔　(b _ s _)
2. accept　　　 ⇔　(ref _ _ e)
3. amateur　　　⇔　(ex _ _ rt)
4. disbelieve　 ⇔　(tr _ _ t)

II Note-taking 🎧 35

本文を聴きながらノートをとりましょう。（英語でも日本語でも構いません）

III Reading Aloud & Shadowing 🎧 36

ＣＤを聴きながら、発音に気をつけて音読をしましょう。次に本を閉じて、シャドーイングしましょう。

1. Another expression for having no real choice is "between a rock and a hard place.
2. It is often used to describe a difficult situation with few choices — none of them good.
3. For example, your boss may ask you to work late.
4. But you have plans to go to a movie with your friends.

IV Reading Comprehension

Reading

① Making choices is necessary, but not always easy. Many of our expressions tell about this difficulty. One of these expressions is "Hobson's choice." It often is used to describe a difficult choice. But that is not what it really means. Its real meaning is to have no choice at all. The Hobson in the expression was Thomas Hobson. Mr. Hobson owned a stable of horses in Cambridge, England. Mr. Hobson often rented horses to the students at Cambridge University. But, he did not really trust them to take good care of the horses. So, he had a rule that prevented the students from riding his best horses. They could take the horse that was nearest the stable door. Or, they could not take any horse at all. Thus, a Hobson's choice was really no choice.

② Another expression for having no real choice is "between a rock and a hard place." It is often used to describe a difficult situation with few choices — none of them good. For example, your boss may ask you to work late. But you have plans to go to a movie with your friends. If you refuse to work, your boss gets angry. But if you do not go to the movies with your friends, *they* may get angry. So what do you do? You are "caught between a rock and a hard place."

③ Another expression — "between the devil and the deep blue sea" — also gives you a choice between two equally dangerous things. Its meaning seems clear. You can choose the devil and his burning fires of hell. Or, you can choose to drown in the sea. Some word experts say the expression comes from the days of wooden ships. The "devil" is a word for a seam between two pieces of wood along the water-line of a ship. If the seam or crack between the two pieces of wood begins to leak, then a sailor must fix it. The sailor ordered to make the repairs was in a dangerous situation. He was hanging over the side of the ship, working "between the devil and the deep blue sea."

❹ There is still another expression that describes a situation with only bad choices — being "on the horns of a dilemma." The dictionary says a dilemma is a situation in which you must make a decision about two equally balanced choices. When your dilemma has horns, a choice becomes impossible. When you are "on the horns of a dilemma" no matter which horn you choose, something bad will happen.

(422 Words)

本文について、下記の設問に答えましょう。

1. The word **prevented** in paragraph 1 is closest in meaning to
   a. hindered
   b. allowed
   c. liberated
   d. released

2. The word **seam** in paragraph 3 is closest in meaning to
   a. appearance
   b. show
   c. joint
   d. opening

3. In paragraph 1, the author says that the true meaning of a Hobson's Choice is
   a. not really having a choice
   b. having a difficult choice
   c. having many choices
   d. making necessary choices

4. According to paragraph 4, what does it mean to be "on the horns of a dilemma"?
   a. It's important to make the right choice.
   b. Your choices are not equal.
   c. All of your possible choices are bad.
   d. You have no choice.

5. In the article, all of the following are mentioned as difficulties EXCEPT

    a. having no real choice
    b. having so many good choices that it's difficult to pick just one
    c. having to choose between two dangerous things
    d. only having choices that will lead to something bad

【Extension Activity 1: timed reading】

1分間でどれだけ読めるか計測してみましょう。

1st time	words	2nd time	words

【Extension Activity 2: typing】

1分間でどれだけタイプできるか計測してみましょう。

1st time	words	2nd time	words

V Integrated Skills 37

What was your favorite subject at school? Describe it and explain why it was your favorite subject.

CDを聴いて、(　　　　　) に記入しましょう。

    (1.　　　　　　　　　　　) was music. I started learning how to play the piano when I was four years old, so I was already familiar with some (2.　　　　　　　　) before I entered (3.　　　　). Music is not among the main subjects in school like (4.　　　　　　) and language learning, but it gave me a lot of (5.　　　　　) as well as (6.　　　　　　) at school. This is (7.　　　　　) why I liked music so much at school.

                                                            (82 words)

【Extension Activity 3: writing】
あなた自身の答えを書いてみましょう。

....
....
....
....
....
....

【Extension Activity 4: speaking】
あなた自身の答えを話してみましょう。

TOEFL® Test Skills

キャンパス用語クイズ （Part 3）

以下は英語圏の大学で学ぶ学問分野の用語です。日本語に相当する英語になるよう、下線部にアルファベットを入れてみましょう。

1. P _ _ sics　　　　　物理学
2. L _ _ 　　　　　　法学
3. P _ _ _ hology　　　心理学
4. Engin _ _ _ ing　　　工学
5. Lit _ _ _ ture　　　　文学
6. Econo _ _ _ s　　　　経済学
7. Computer S _ _ _ nce　コンピュータサイエンス

Unit 13 Baloney

① Words and Phrases

この章で学ぶ表現を確認しましょう。

A 語群からもっとも適切な５つの語句を選びましょう。

1. 政権　　　（　　　　　）　2. 知事　（　　　　　）
3. 司教・司祭（　　　　　）　4. 城主　（　　　　　）
5. 軍隊　　　（　　　　　）

governor　troops　lord　bishop　administration

B 左側の日本語の意味にあてはまる表現を選び、書きましょう。

1. 言い訳をする　　　（　　　　　　　）
2. 人に信じ込ませる　（　　　　　　　）
3. さかのぼる　　　　（　　　　　　　）

make excuses　go back to　make someone believe

II. Note-taking 🎧 38

本文を聴きながらノートをとりましょう。（英語でも日本語でも構いません）

III. Reading Aloud & Shadowing 🎧 39

ＣＤを聴きながら、発音に気をつけて音読をしましょう。次に本を閉じて、シャドーイングしましょう。

1. Another expression is pulling the wool over someone's eyes.
2. It means to make someone believe something that is not true.
3. The expression goes back to the days when men wore false hair or wigs.
4. The word wool was a popular joking word for hair.

IV. Reading Comprehension

① Baloney is a kind of sausage that many Americans eat often. (1) The word also has another meaning in English. It is used to describe something — usually something someone says — that is false or wrong or foolish. Baloney sausage comes from the name of the Italian city, Bologna. (2) But, baloney sausage does not taste the same as beef or pork alone. Some language experts think this different taste is responsible for the birth of the expression baloney. (3) Baloney is an idea or statement that is nothing like the truth, in the same way that baloney sausage tastes nothing like the meat that is used to make it. (4)

② Baloney is a word often used by politicians to describe the ideas of their opponents. The expression has been used for years. A former governor of New York state, Alfred Smith, criticized some claims by President Franklin Roosevelt about the successes of the Roosevelt administration. Smith said, "No matter how thin you slice it, it is still baloney."

③ A similar word has almost the same meaning as baloney. It even sounds almost the same. The word is blarney. It began in Ireland in about sixteen hundred. The lord of Blarney castle, near Cork, agreed to surrender the castle to British troops. But he kept making excuses for postponing the surrender. And, he made them sound like very good excuses, "this is just more of the same blarney." The Irish castle now is famous for its Blarney stone. Kissing the stone is thought to give a person special powers of speech. One who has kissed the Blarney stone, so the story goes, can speak words of praise so smoothly and sweetly that you believe them, even when you know they are false. A former Roman Catholic bishop of New York City, Fulton Sheen, once explained, "Baloney is praise so thick it cannot be true. And blarney is praise so thin we like it."

④ Another expression is pulling the wool over someone's eyes. It means to make someone believe something that is not true. The expression goes back to the days when men wore false hair, or wigs, similar to those worn by judges today in British courts. The word wool was a popular joking word for hair. If you pulled a man's wig over his eyes, he could not see what was happening. Today, when you pull the wool over someone's eyes, he cannot see the truth.

(406 Words)

本文について、下記の設問に答えましょう。

1. The word **alone** in paragraph 1 is closest in meaning to

   a. lonely
   b. peerless
   c. unequally
   d. solely

2. The word **former** in paragraph 2 is closest in meaning to

   a. current
   b. following
   c. ex-
   d. legal

3. Look at the four numbers that indicate where the following sentence could be added to paragraph 1.

   The city is famous for its sausage, a mixture of smoked, spiced meat from cows and pigs.

   Where would the sentence best fit?

   a. (1)   **b.** (2)   **c.** (3)   **d.** (4)

4. According to paragraph 3, what happens if you kiss the Blarney stone?

   a. You'll become a sweeter person.
   b. You'll never believe anything.
   c. You'll be praised by everybody.
   d. You'll become a smooth speaker.

5. In the article, all of the following are linked to untruths EXCEPT

  a. a type of animal   **b.** a type of material
  c. a type of food   **d.** a type of rock

【Extension Activity 1: timed reading】

1分間でどれだけ読めるか計測してみましょう。

| 1st time   words | 2nd time   words |

【Extension Activity 2: typing】

1分間でどれだけタイプできるか計測してみましょう。

| 1st time   words | 2nd time   words |

V Integrated Skills 40

What is your favorite kind of food? Describe it and explain why it is your favorite.

CD を聴いて、(   ) に記入しましょう。

My favorite food is Thai green curry. Curries in Thailand are different from curries (1.   ). (2.   ) are curry paste, coconut milk, meat, seafood, and vegetables. Thai green curry (3.   ) using herbs and green chilies, which make the dish look "green." When you eat the green curry, the coconut milk and herbs (4.   ). It is also (5.   ), so why don't you try (6.   ) and enjoy a dish that is (7.   )?

(86 words)

82   TOEFL iBT® Basics

【Extension Activity 3: writing】
あなた自身の答えを書いてみましょう。

_____
_____
_____
_____
_____
_____

【Extension Activity 4: speaking】
あなた自身の答えを話してみましょう。

TOEFL® Test Skills

Integrated Skills の鍛え方

四技能の総合力が求められます。まずはreading、listeningを鍛えましょう。

speaking、writingでも、まず英語の会話や講義、テキストを聞いたり読んだりした後に、それについて話したり書いたりすることが求められます。よく聞き、素早く読んで理解し、論点をつかんでからでないと答えられません。

たとえ細かい点や単語が分からなくても、辞書なしで聞いて読んで、素早く内容の大意をつかむことができるよう、「多読多聴」を心がけましょう。

Unit 14　Mayday

I　Words and Phrases

この章で学ぶ表現を確認しましょう。

A 語群からもっとも適切な5つの語句を選びましょう。

1. 致死的な、命にかかわる (　　　　　　　)　2. 犯罪　(　　　　　　　)
3. 転覆　(　　　　　　　)　　　　　　　　4. 殺人　(　　　　　　　)
5. 食欲　(　　　　　　　)

appetite　　life-threatening　　subversion　　murder　　crime

B 左側の日本語の意味にあてはまる表現を選び、書きましょう。

1. そのままにしておく　　(　　　　　　　　　)
2. 〜とは関係がない　　　(　　　　　　　　　)
3. 時代の先を行く　　　　(　　　　　　　　　)

nothing to do with　　leave 〜 alone　　ahead of its time

84　TOEFL iBT® Basics

II. Note-taking 🎧 41

本文を聴きながらノートをとりましょう。（英語でも日本語でも構いません）

III. Reading Aloud & Shadowing 🎧 42

ＣＤを聴きながら、発音に気をつけて音読をしましょう。次に本を閉じて、シャドーイングしましょう。

1. Many French words are used in the arts.
2. For example, a "film noir" is a movie about murder and other crimes.
3. These films were popular in the 1940s and 1950s.
4. Anything in art, music or literature which is very modern or ahead of its time is called "avant-garde."

IV Reading Comprehension

Reading

❶ (1) "Mayday" is an emergency code word. It is used around the world in voice communications. (2) You might see a war movie in which an airplane has been hit by rocket fire. (3) Mayday has nothing to do with the month of May. (4) It comes from the French expressions "venez m'aider," or "m'aidez," which mean "help me."

❷ Frederick Stanley Mockford created the mayday call signal in the 1920s. Mockford was a radio officer at Croydon Airport in London. He was asked to think of a word that could be used in an emergency. The word had to be easily understood by all pilots and airport workers. Much of the air traffic at that time was between Croydon Airport and Le Bourget Airport near Paris, France. So he proposed the word "mayday." Today, many groups use the word to mean a life-threatening emergency. The call is always given three times to prevent mistaking it for some similar sounding words.

❸ Many other French words are commonly used in English. One of these words is even in the Special English Word Book. It is "sabotage." It means "to damage or destroy as an act of subversion against an organization or nation." You may have heard the term "laissez-faire" to describe a kind of economic or political policy. It means "to leave alone and not interfere." It was first used in France in the 18th century.

❹ In the business world, "entrepreneur" is another French word. It means a person who starts and operates a new business and has responsibility for any risks involved. Many French words are used in the arts. For example, a "film noir" is a movie about murder and other crimes. These films were popular in the 1940s and 1950s. Anything in art, music or literature which is very modern or ahead of its time is called "avant-garde." If you are looking for a job, you must prepare your resumé. This document lists all of your education, skills and experience.

❺ Something that is one of a kind and like no other thing is called "unique." The French are famous for their food. All cooks need to know how to sauté. This is frying something quickly in a small amount of oil or butter. When you are eating at a restaurant, the server may tell you "bon appétit," which means "good appetite," or "enjoy your meal." And if you go away, someone may wish you "bon voyage," or "have a good trip."

(412 Words)

本文について、下記の設問に答えましょう。

1. The word **proposed** in paragraph 2 is closest in meaning to
   a. dissuaded
   b. refused
   c. abducted
   d. suggested

2. The word **interfere** in paragraph 3 refers to
   a. benefit
   b. facilitate
   c. impede
   d. improvise

3. Look at the four numbers that indicate where the following sentence could be added to paragraph 1.

   The pilot gets on his radio and calls "mayday, mayday, mayday" to tell that his plane is in danger of crashing to the ground.

   Where would the sentence best fit?
   a. (1)
   b. (2)
   c. (3)
   d. (4)

4. According to paragraph 2, which of the following sentences is true?
   a. Frederick Mockford was in an emergency in the 1920s.
   b. Frederick Mockford was looking for a word that could be understood by French people only.
   c. The word "mayday" is not used very often these days.
   d. You must say the word "mayday" more than once so that it isn't confused with other words.

5. What do you need if you are looking for work?

   a. your resumé
   b. your entrepreneur
   c. your avant-garde
   d. your sabotage

【Extension Activity 1: timed reading】
1 分間でどれだけ読めるか計測してみましょう。

| 1st time | words | 2nd time | words |

【Extension Activity 2: typing】
1 分間でどれだけタイプできるか計測してみましょう。

| 1st time | words | 2nd time | words |

V Integrated Skills 🎧 43

Some people prefer to eat out. Other people prefer to cook and eat food at home. Which do you prefer?

CD を聴いて、(   ) に記入しましょう。

I prefer to (1.   ). There are three reasons for this. Firstly, they not only offer a variety of food and drink but also (2.   ) to dine in. I can relax and feel at home, especially in those places I like. Secondly, they provide a good chance to (3.   ). Someone that you meet there might become (4.   ). Finally, eating out surely saves time on (5.   ), such as (6.   ). That is why I prefer to eat out rather than (7.   ).

(99 words)

【Extension Activity 3: writing】
あなた自身の答えを書いてみましょう。

【Extension Activity 4: speaking】
あなた自身の答えを話してみましょう。

TOEFL® Test Skills

ニュース用語クイズ

以下は国際ニュースでよく使われる単語・表現です。あてはまるものを選び、書きましょう。

1. 児童虐待　　　（　　　　　　　　　　）
2. 人種差別　　　（　　　　　　　　　　）
3. 生涯教育　　　（　　　　　　　　　　）
4. 核家族　　　　（　　　　　　　　　　）
5. 青少年非行　　（　　　　　　　　　　）

| lifelong education | child abuse | juvenile delinquency |
| nuclear family | racial discrimination | |

Unit 15 — Without Them, Machines Fall Apart

I. Words and Phrases

この章で学ぶ表現を確認しましょう。

A 語群からもっとも適切な5つの語句を選びましょう。

1. 議長　　（　　　　　）　　2. 上院議員　（　　　　　）
3. 下院議員（　　　　　）　　4. 大使　　　（　　　　　）
5. 首相　　（　　　　　）

ambassador　　senator　　congressman　　chairman　　prime minister

B 左側の定義にあてはまる英単語を選びましょう。

1. the activity of managing the relationships between countries
（　　　　　）
2. the process or business of taking goods from one place to another
（　　　　　）
3. an amount of something that is available to be used　（　　　　　）
4. someone who is in a position of authority in an organization
（　　　　　）

transport　　supply　　official　　diplomacy

II Note-taking 🎧44

本文を聴きながらノートをとりましょう。（英語でも日本語でも構いません）

III Reading Aloud & Shadowing 🎧45

ＣＤを聴きながら、発音に気をつけて音読をしましょう。次に本を閉じて、シャドーイングしましょう。

1. In a military operation, strategy decisions are important.
2. But much more time is spent on the nuts and bolts — generally called logistics — of how to transport and supply an army.
3. It has been said that Napoleon was successful because he knew the field position of every one of his guns.
4. He gave careful attention to the nuts and bolts of his operations.

IV Reading Comprehension

❶ Every machine is held together by its nuts and bolts. Without them, the machine would fall apart. That is also true of an organization. Its nuts and bolts are its basic, necessary elements. They are the parts that make the organization work. In government, industry, diplomacy — in most anything — those who understand the nuts and bolts are the most important. Success depends more on them than on almost anyone else.

❷ (1) In government, the president or prime minister may plan and shape programs and policies. But, it takes much more work to get them approved and to make them successful. (2) There is a mass of detailed work to be done — the nuts and bolts. This is often put into the hands of specialists. The top leaders are always well-known, but not those who work with the nuts and bolts. This is equally true in the day-to-day operation of Congress. (3) The majority leader of the Senate and the Speaker of the House of Representatives — together with the chairmen of committees — keep the business of Congress moving. Behind every Senator and Congressman, however, are assistants. (4)

❸ In diplomacy, the chief ministers are unquestionably important in negotiations. But there are lesser officials who do the basic work and preparations on the different issues to be negotiated. A recent book tells of a British prime minister who decided to send an ambassador to Washington to learn if details could be worked out for joint action on an issue. The talks in Washington, the minister said, would be "of nuts and bolts." He meant, of course, the talks would concern all the necessary elements to make joint action successful.

❹ In a military operation, strategy decisions are important. But much more time is spent on the nuts and bolts — generally called logistics — of how to transport and supply an army. It has been said that Napoleon was successful because he knew the field position of every one of his guns. He gave careful attention to the nuts and bolts of his operations.

❺ The extreme importance of nuts and bolts was expressed by the Elizabethan poet, George Herbert. He wrote:

For want of a nail, the shoe is lost.
For want of a shoe, the horse is lost.
For want of a horse, the rider is lost.

Benjamin Franklin carried these lines even further. He wrote:

For want of a rider, the battle was lost.
For want of a battle, the kingdom was lost.
And all for the want of a horseshoe nail.

(418 Words)

本文について、下記の設問に答えましょう。

1. The word **elements** in paragraph 1 is closest in meaning to

　a. solutions　　**b.** complex　　**c.** spirits　　**d.** factors

2. The word **strategy** in paragraph 4 is closest in meaning to

　a. statistics　　**b.** tactics　　**c.** figures　　**d.** demography

3. Look at the four numbers that indicate where the following sentence could be added to paragraph 2.

These people do all the detailed work to prepare congressmen to vote wisely on each issue.

Where would the sentence best fit?

　a. (1)　　**b.** (2)　　**c.** (3)　　**d.** (4)

4. In paragraph 5, the main message of the two poems is best summarized by which of the following sentences?
   a. Horses should not be used in battle.
   b. Missing one small thing can have a large effect.
   c. You shouldn't ride a horse without a shoe.
   d. Small details are not important in war.

5. According to the article, the following are all correct EXCEPT
   a. The nuts and bolts are the most important element of any organization.
   b. In government, a large amount of work is done behind the scenes.
   c. Chief ministers are not needed in diplomatic negotiations.
   d. Napoleon was successful because he paid attention to details.

【Extension Activity 1: timed reading】
1分間でどれだけ読めるか計測してみましょう。

| 1st time | words | 2nd time | words |

【Extension Activity 2: typing】
1分間でどれだけタイプできるか計測してみましょう。

| 1st time | words | 2nd time | words |

V Integrated Skills 46

Where is your favorite place to study? Describe this place and say why it is a good place for you to study.

CDを聴いて、(　　　　　) に記入しましょう。

My favorite place to study is (1.　　　　　　　　). I often go there after classes are over. (2.　　　　　　), it is very quiet, so I can (3.　　　　　　) my study without any interruption. (4.　　　　　　), a lot of information is available in the library. I can search the database (5.　　　　　　). (6.　　　　　　), the library offers many services concerning IT training. The university library is (7.　　　　　　) to obtain broad knowledge and skills for the future.

(84 words)

94　TOEFL iBT® Basics

【Extension Activity 3: writing】
あなた自身の答えを書いてみましょう。

....
....
....
....
....
....

【Extension Activity 4: speaking】
あなた自身の答えを話してみましょう。

TOEFL® Test Skills

時間に十分余裕をもって申し込みをしましょう。

TOEFL iBT® テストは全国の指定の受験場所で年に50回以上行われていますが、コンピュータの台数に限りがあります。入室の際に写真、署名入りの身分証明書（パスポート）の提示が求められるので、あらかじめ取得しておく必要があります。身分証明書（パスポート）の期限切れにも注意しましょう。

また、日本だけではなく近隣諸国からの受験生が受験に来ることもあります。時間に余裕を持って申し込まないと、席が全て埋まっていて予定していた日時までに受験できなくなる可能性もあるため、注意しましょう。

[出典]

Unit 1	From Couch Potato to Cabin Fever	

http://learningenglish.voanews.com/content/words-and-their-stories-from-couch-potato-to-cabin-fever-132322483/118835.html

Unit 2　Fireworks!
http://learningenglish.voanews.com/content/fireworks-diwali-washington/1686081.html

Unit 3　We Put Things in "Apple Pie Order"
http://learningenglish.voanews.com/content/apple-pie-order/1715059.html

Unit 4　The Big Easy and Sin City
http://learningenglish.voanews.com/content/new-orleans-big-easy-jazz-las-vegas-elvis-presley/1734084.html

Unit 5　Bigwig
http://learningenglish.voanews.com/content/a-23-2007-04-09-voa4-83131767/126811.html

Unit 6　Grapevine
http://learningenglish.voanews.com/content/heard-it-through-the-grapevine/1860426.html

Unit 7　Quit Buggin' Me!
http://learningenglish.voanews.com/content/insects-bees-butterflies-bedbugs/1760825.html

Unit 8　It's Not Worth a Hill of Beans!
http://learningenglish.voanews.com/content/hill-beans-farm-expressions-hay-hedging/1781071.html

Unit 9　What's a GI Joe?
http://learningenglish.voanews.com/content/leatherneck-grunt-doughboy-gijoe-marines/1873092.html

Unit 10　Great Scott
http://learningenglish.voanews.com/content/words-and-their-stories-great-scott/1499918.html

Unit 11　Swan Song
http://learningenglish.voanews.com/content/words-and-their-stories-swan-song-128818748/118823.html

Unit 12　When Is a Choice Not Really a Choice?
http://learningenglish.voanews.com/content/hobsons-choice-between-a-rock-and-a-hard-place/1820856.html

Unit 13　Baloney
http://learningenglish.voanews.com/content/words-and-their-stories-baloney-148315935/608028.html

Unit 14　Mayday
http://learningenglish.voanews.com/content/words-and-their-stories-mayday-149363765/606730.html

Unit 15　Without Them, Machines Fall Apart
http://learningenglish.voanews.com/content/nuts-and-bolts-details-logistics-napoleon/1820887.html

Glossary

A		
administration	the government of a country at a particular time	政権
agricultural	relating to the practice of farming	農業の
(the) Allies	the group of countries that fought together in the First and Second World Wars	連合国、同盟国
ambassador	an important official who represents his or her government in a foreign country	大使
ant	a small wingless insect, often with a sting, that lives in large groups	蟻
appetite	a desire for food	食欲
arrest	to take someone to a police station because he or she may have committed a crime.	逮捕する

B		
bedbug	a small insect that lives especially in beds where it bites people and sucks their blood	なんきんむし、トコジラミ
bet	the money that you risk on a future event	賭け金
bishop	a high-ranked priest in Christianity	司教、司祭

C		
campaign	a series of activities to win an election	選挙運動
candidate	a person who is nominated for election	候補者
chairman	someone who is in charge of a meeting	議長
citizen	a person who lives in a particular town, country or state	市民
cocoon	a covering of silk threads that some insects make to protect themselves before they become adults	繭
commander	an officer of any rank who is in charge of soldiers	司令官、命令者

competition	a situation in which people try to be more successful than others	競争
condition	the state of something; a rule or decision that you must agree to	状態、条件
congressman	a politician who is a member of the U.S. House of Representatives	米国連邦議会下院議員
container	something such as a box that can be used to keep or transport something	容器
crack	a very narrow space between two things	裂け目
crescent	a curved shape that is wider in the middle and pointed at each end	三日月形
crime	illegal activities	犯罪
criminal	a person who has committed a crime	犯罪者
cursor	a small mark that can be moved around a computer screen to show where you are working or where text will be added	[コンピュータ]カーソル

D

defence	the lawyer or lawyers whose job is to prove in court that a person did not commit a crime	被告側
describe	to say in detail what something or someone is like	記述する、描写する
device	a piece of equipment that has been designed for a particular purpose	装置、工夫
drown	to die from being underwater for too long, or to kill someone in this way	溺れさせる、溺死する

E

experiment	a scientific test done to study what happens and to gain new ideas	実験
explode	to burst, or to make something burst into pieces with a loud noise	爆発する
explorer	someone who travels to unknown places to find out more about them	探検家

F

fail	to be unsuccessful	失敗する
far-off	a long way from where you are	はるかかなたの
fix	to put something firmly in a particular place; to repair something	固定させる、修理する

G

galvanized	covered with zinc	亜鉛メッキされた
governor	a person who is the official head of a region	知事、統治者
grain	the seeds of crops such as wheat, corn, or rice	穀物

H

hard-earned	having taken a great deal of effort to acquire	骨を折ってもうけた
hive	a small box for bees to live in	ミツバチの巣箱
hold	to carry or to have something in your hand; to make something stay in a particular position	手に持つ、保持する
honor	high respect	名誉
hornet	a large black and yellow flying insect that has a powerful sting	ススメバチ

J

judge	the official in a court who decides if and how criminals should be punished	裁判官

K

knee	the joint between the top and bottom parts of the leg	ひざ

L

land	the surface of the earth that is not sea	陸地
life-threatening	potentially fatal	生命をあやうくする
lord	someone having power who owned a lot of land in the past	君主、主人

Glossary

M		
march	to walk in a military manner	行進する
(the) Marines	a branch of the U.S. military	海兵隊
mayor	the head of a city	市長
murder	the crime of killing someone	殺人
mythology	legends, folkstories, or folklore	神話
N		
nomination	the act of choosing somebody as a candidate in an election	指名、推薦
O		
operation	an organized activity involving a number of people	操作、作戦、活動
opponent	a person that you are playing or fighting against in a competition, battle, etc.	競争相手、反対者
P		
philosopher	a person who thinks deeply about things	哲学者
poet	a person who writes poems	詩人
postpone	to change the date or time of a planned event, etc. to a later time or date	延期する
presidency	the job or period of being president	大統領の地位、任期
prime minister	the head of an elected government	首相
R		
religious	relating to a belief in one or more gods	宗教上の、宗教的な
remove	to take something away from a place	取り去る、取り除く
rent	a tenant's regular payment to a landlord	家賃
S		
senator	a member of the US Senate	（米）上院議員
stable	a building where horses are kept	馬小屋
subversion	effort to change management, direction, or control	転覆

T

telegraph	a method of sending messages using electrical signals	電信、電報
term	a word or phrase; a period; one of the three periods in the school year	用語、学期、期間
trader	a person whose job is to buy and sell	貿易業者
troop	soldier or member of the armed forces	軍隊

V

vice president	the person who is next in rank to the president of a country	副大統領
vote	to show which person you want to win an election, or which idea you support by marking a piece of paper or raising your hand	投票する

W

wage	money you earn that is typically paid on an hourly, daily or weekly basis	賃金
work late	to work after the time you usually finish	残業する

Timed Reading (wpm) Record Sheet

Unit	1st time		2nd time	
	date	wpm	date	wpm
1				
2				
3				
4				
5				
6				
7				
8				
9				
10				
11				
12				
13				
14				
15				

Typing (wpm) Record Sheet

Unit	1ˢᵗ time		2ⁿᵈ time	
	date	wpm	date	wpm
1				
2				
3				
4				
5				
6				
7				
8				
9				
10				
11				
12				
13				
14				
15				

> 著作権法上，無断複写・複製は禁じられています。

TOEFL iBT® Basics　　　　　　　　　　　　　　　　[B-786]
TOEFL iBT®テストスキル入門　～VOAで学ぶ四技能のストラテジー～

第1刷	2015年3月10日
第2刷	2020年3月30日

著　者	津田　晶子	Akiko Tsuda
	クリストファー・ヴァルヴォーナ	Chris Valvona
	金志　佳代子	Kayoko Kinshi
	岩本　弓子	Yumiko Iwamoto

発行者　南雲一範　Kazunori Nagumo
発行所　株式会社　南雲堂
　　　　〒162-0801　東京都新宿区山吹町361
　　　　NAN'UN-DO Publishing Co., Ltd.
　　　　361 Yamabuki-cho, Shinjuku-ku, Tokyo 162-0801, Japan
　　　　振替口座：00160-0-46863
　　　　TEL: 03-3268-2311（代表）／FAX: 03-3269-2486

編集者	丸小　雅臣
英文校閲	ケリー・マクドナルド　Kelly MacDonald
表　紙	奥定　泰之
組　版	Office haru
装　丁	Nスタジオ
検　印	省　略
コード	ISBN978-4-523-17786-9　C0082

Printed in Japan

落丁・乱丁，その他不良品がございましたら，お取り替えいたします。

E-mail　nanundo@post.email.ne.jp
URL　http://www.nanun-do.co.jp/